DEAR GOD

Children on Happiness

The Best Christmas Presents Are Wrapped in Heaven (with Elizabeth Heller)

Grandparents Are Made for Hugging (with Elizabeth Heller)

Fathers Are Like Elephants Because They're the Biggest Ones Around (But They Still Are Pretty Gentle Underneath)

My Mother Is the Best Gift I Ever Got

Love Is Like a Crayon Because It Comes in All Colors

Just Build the Ark and the Animals Will Come: Children on Bible Stories

Growing Up Isn't Hard to Do If You Start Out as a Kid

"Mr. President, Why Don't You Paint Your White House Another Color!"

Talking to Your Child About God: A Book for Families of All Faiths

Dear God, What Religion Were the Dinosaurs?

The Children's God

DEAR GOD
Children's Letters
to God

DAVID HELLER, Ph.D.

Illustrated by John Alcorn

A PERIGEE BOOK

A Perigee Book
Published by
The Berkley Publishing Group
200 Madison Avenue
New York, NY 10016

First published in hardcover by Doubleday in 1987.
First Perigee edition: December 1994.

Library of Congress Cataloging-in-Publication Data
Dear God : children's letters to God / [compiled by] David Heller :
   illustrated by John Alcorn.
        p.   cm.
   "A Perigee book."
   ISBN 0-399-52142-9 (alk. paper)
   1. Children—Religious life.   2. God.   3. Imaginary letters.
I. Heller, David.
[BL625.5.D43   1994]
231'.083—dc20   94-6938
                                                               CIP

Cover design by Keith Sheridan Associates, Inc.
Cover illustration by Annmari Olsson
Printed in the United States of America
1   2   3   4   5   6   7   8   9   10

This book is printed on acid-free paper.

To my wife, Elizabeth,
who I met while preparing
Dear God and who shares
in my love for God
and passion for
spiritual reflection
and humor

✵

Contents

❧

Introduction

As a child I thought as a child, but I was drawn to the global concerns of adults. I wanted to make sense of how people acted, and I was especially curious about belief and doubt in a God. I asked many questions of nearby grownups, local clergy, and teachers as well as my parents. "Why is the world the way it is?" I asked with tireless persistence. I received many different answers, as most children do, and I kept searching. A few years later, I became one of the first Jews in a private, Jesuit Catholic high school. This experience, particularly the close relationships I developed with faculty and friends, continued my fascination with the religions of the world. By 1984, after studying psychology and religion at Harvard and Michigan, respectively, the topic of children's God images formally became a part of my life. It was then that I began writing *The*

Children's God, a book published in 1986 by the University of Chicago Press.

Writing this book helped me to understand other people's religious views as well as my own. Through my research for the book, I found that children share many ideas about God despite their differences in religion, age, and gender. Most children are concerned with how powerful God is and whether God will be a significant force in their lives. They believe that God is all around, in the sky, in flowers, and in people too. They talk a great deal about "the God in people." These small theologians express clear interest in their spiritual relationship to their neighbors. They seem to conclude that God created the human race with a purpose in mind, and that we are all connected to that purpose and to each other. As twelve-year-old Tamara described, "It's all woven together . . . All of our lives . . . And God is at the center of our world, guiding our destiny."

While children's ideas about God should be seriously considered, they can also be lightheartedly enjoyed. While I was completing *The Children's God*, I collected a great variety of original drawings,

stories, conversations, and letters. I was particularly
moved by the children's letters. I also received mail
from parents of a variety of religious backgrounds,
including devout churchgoers and atheistic parents.
They were simply responding to my work with children and wanted to offer a letter or an anecdote.
The humor and vitality that leaped forth from so
many of their children's original and spontaneous
ideas were undeniable. I found myself collecting
more letters from other children and sharing the
letters with friends and relatives, including my thir-
teen-year-old and ten-year-old cousins. Adults and
children alike seemed to lose themselves in what
can only be described as "a childlike sense of wonder and laughter." I knew I must share this colorful
parade of letters with a larger audience. One by one,
the children's letters provide inspiration for all of us.

Children write to God about all different kinds of
things. Full of curiosities, dreams, and stories to
tell, children have a wonderful knack for sharing
their innermost thoughts in their letters. Some children write at length about everyday concerns—
about mom and dad, brothers and sisters, school ac-
tivities and challenges, and the ups and downs of

friendship and play. Family themes are especially vivid since parents play the primary role in helping to develop a child's God image. Some youngsters write to God about the world at large—about international troubles and national leadership, the way men and women act with each other, and those sometimes fuzzy ideas we get from television and movies. Even more than when I was a child in the 1960s, the media seem to have a profound influence on children's notions of good forces and bad forces, heroes and supernatural characters. But some children are even more reflective. They're sincerely curious about really "hard-to-explain" things—like science, nature, and religious belief and doubt. The teachings of the Bible and established religions are frequently apparent in the letters, though these formal influences tend to emerge in humorous and even exaggerated ways. Whatever an individual child's interests, we can be certain that he or she will be quite outspoken and animated—for that is what childhood is all about.

For me, personally, there have been quite a few stops on the journey from curious child to curious interviewer of children. Most recently, I interviewed youngsters concerning the Bible and published *Just Build the Ark and the Animals Will Come*. Yet some things have remained the same: Religion conveys for me a great joy and lightness of spirit and children are the ideal messengers of that spirit. So please join me in enjoying the timeless spirit of children. It is my considerable pleasure to pass along their letters to God and share with you their sweetness.

DAVID HELLER, Ph.D.

Boston, Massachusetts

"Did You Think That Christmas Would Turn out Like This When You Started It?"

Dear God,
Did you think that Christmas would turn out like this when you started it?

Love,
Wendy
[age 7]

Dear God,
Do you have a favorite religion? I'll give you three to choose from—

1. Catholic
2. Lutheran
3. Episcapalin

Best wishes,
Charles
[age 10]

P.S. I'm Episcapalin.

Dear God,
   I think you must be real smart to invent religion.
That way you get all the people to look up to you
and say your name a lot. I want to be famous too.
My names's Frank.

Yours truly,
Frank ✡ ✡ ✡
[age 11]

Dear God,
   Does Pat Robertson really know you personally?
If not, I thought you should know that he talks
about you a lot.

Your friend
Brent
[age 8]

God,
   What's the story? Why did you make the Jews
stay in the desert for 40 years?

Keith
[age 7]

Dear God,

In school, I drew a picture of Jesus and the 12 disciplens. If you want to see my drawing, stop by my house at 7 tonight.

Love,
Jennifer
[age 9]

Dear God,

Your my favorite God. I don't have anybody before you. I praise you a lot. I hope you will write me back and think of me always. Call me if you want.

Love,
Jerry
[age 9]

Dear God,

How old are you? If that Noah story is right, you must be older than my neighbor, Mr. Grubb—and he's really old.

Take it easy,
Tammy
[age 8]

Dear God,

Can't you make church more fun? What about having a few videos?

Just trying to help,
Celia
[age 10]

Dear God,

Why did you give Jesus such a hard time? My dad is rough on me too. So I know what it's like. Maybe you both could ease up?

Mark
[age 11]

Dear God,

Do you have a few minutes? I have a few things to say. First, thank you for the bike for Christmas. Second, thanks for the snow. Third, how about more holidays?

Sincerely,
Angela
[age 9]

Dear God,

I live in a very religious place, but you already no that because you visited. What I want to know is was New York City a mistake? Please tell the truth. We'll keep it a secret.

Love,
Jamie
[age 8]

Dear God,

Who do *you* pray to? If you don't say prayers, do you think you can let me off the hook?

Jim
[age 9]

Dear God,

I love you. I just want to let you know ahead of time that I'd like to be there with you in heaven.

Love always,
Sarah
[age 8]

Dear God,
    Why is the cross ✝ the thing you chose for religion?
    We (my friend Jody and me) think you should have tried something different.
    How about something like this? ⚭

> Have a nice day,
> Pearl
> [age 11]

We hope no one has used this before.

Dear God,
    If the Lions were as wimpy back in bible times as the ones here are, the Christians would have won.
    The Lions are a football team if you did not know it.

> I hope that you are not
> bothered by this,
> Chuck
> [age 10]

Dear God,

What religion are the people in London? Have they got Christianity yet?

Anna
[age 8]

Dear God,

I just learned how to spell R E L I G I O N.

I feel good. Now I am learning something else that we are. It is called P R E S S B U T A R R I U N.

Emily
[age 6]

Dear God,

How are you doing? I heard that you had a cold. But keep the faith. We are working on a cure.

Best wishes,
Dr. Tony
[age 11]

Dear God,

What do you *really* think about atheists? I think that you must feel like I feel about the Yankees—I hate them.

> Tom
> [age 9]

Dear God,

I'd like to make a suggestion, if that's okay. Why don't you have fewer religions so peole would get along better? We just read about the Crusades a long time ago.

> Janet
> [age 11]

Dear God,

What do you think about people who convert? My mom says they're stupid. By the way, I like being Jewish.

> Love,
> Amy
> [age 10]

Dear God,
   How did you get to know Mary?
Andy
[age 6]

Dear God,
   Your burning bush trick is better than Doug Henning. I like your act.
Ron
[age 11]

"Is Jesus Your Oldest Kid?"

Dear God,

My dad get laid off last week at work. Please help him find work quick.

He bugs us a lot when he is home.

Thank you,
Martin
[age 8]

Dear nice god,

I feel close to you. Like you and I are part of the same family.

Maybe we could get married and make it easier.

Your lover,
Tina
[age 7]

Dear God, father of Jesus,

How does it feel to be the biggest, best dad in the whole United States?

You must make out okay on father's day.

Bruce
[age 10]

Dear God,
    My grandma died a year ago. My mom says she is with you. Could you give her this letter?
    Here is the letter:
        Grandma, I'm doing good in school and I met a boy I'm going to marry.
                                All my love,
                                Cindy
                                [age 8]

Dear God,
    Thank you for my parents, my sister Anita, and for my grandma and grandpa. They are all real warm and special. I forgive you for my brother Phil. I guess you didn't finish working on him.
                                Sean
                                [age 12]

God,
My father reads to me from your book all the time. I like times when he does.

The Joseph character is interesting.

> Love,
> Joe
> [age 10]

Dear God,
Do you have an extra plague for my sister. Like you did to the Egyptians.

She's real stupid.

> Stanley
> [age 8]

Dear God,
Thank you for the nice weather last week. We had some cousins visiting us. They are from Ohio. That is far away.

I wish you could move Ohio closer to us.

> Jennifer
> [age 7]

Dear God,

My mom is Jewish and my dad is Catholic. My mom says this makes us even more special. Two is better than one.

Do you like to mix things up like this?

See you on all the holidays.

Love you,
Beth
[age 9]

Dear God,

My dad thinks he is you. Please straighten him out.

Wayne
[age 11]

Dear God,

My mom is acting weird because she is getting old. Can you take back a few gray hairs? That would help bring the house back to normal.

Thanks for what you can do.

Mike
[age 9]

Dear Mr. and Mrs. God,
   What's your family like? Is Jesus the oldest?
                                    Karen
                                    [age 7]

Dear God, Esq.
   My family, the Sandersons, is pleased to invite
your family, the Gods, over for bread and wine (I
figured you might like this).
   You are hereby invited on November the 3, at 7
pm.
   Please respond in writing or on a tablet by this
date.
                              Very truly yours,
                              Sheila Sanderson
                              Host
                              [age 11]

Dear God,
Are you in charge of babies?
I have three sisters, which is good. But I would like to put in an order for a brother.
I hope this special order won't upset you.

> Love,
> Stuart
> [age 9]

Dear God,
What is it like at your house? Do you have an address?
My mom says that when you're with God (you), you're always in 7 Heaven.
Is that were I should write to you?

> Love and kindness,
> all the time
> Angela
> 19 Doe Lane
> [age 9]

Dear God,
   This is my family.

Now how about a picture of your family?
                              Brenda
                              [age 6]

Dear God,
   What do you do with families that don't have much faith?
   There's a family on the next block like that. I don't want to get them in trouble. I don't want to say who.
                    See you in church,
                    Alexis
                    [age 9]

Dear God,

My Uncle George is from New Jersey. He tells silly jokes and teases me a lot.

I want to ask—are uncles around so that we will like are parents even more?

Your friend,
Scotty
[age 7]

Dear God,

Was there anything special about Bethlehem, or did you just figure that was as good a place as any to start a franchise?

Your friend,
Jim
[age 12]

Dear God,
   Was there really a Garden of Eden?
   My family has a garden too. But it is small and crummy. It just has a few rotten vegetables.
   Don't tell my mother I said this please.
                                        Larry
                                        [age 10]

Dear God,
   My sister Tina has a girlfriend named Wendy. They are both 15. Wendy has the biggest mouth in the world. No fooling.
   It would take a miracle to shut Wendy up. Got any left?
                                        I'm no tattletale,
                                        Tammy
                                        [age 9]

Dear God,

My mom smokes too much. We are all worried about her health. Even the surgeon general. Help her to stop, please.

Why did you make cigarettes anyway? Was that the Devil's work?

Lori Ann
[age 11]

Dear Father of the universe,

Since the whole galaxy is yours you must have a great family barbecue!

Invite me.
Chip
[age 11]

꧁

Dear God,

Thank you for giving me to a loving and caring family. That was a choice that was a good one.

By the way as long as I'm writing to you. Was there other families that you tried out first?

Take it easy,
Tito
[age 10]

To God,

If everybody in the whole world is related to everybody else, then how can people get married?

Let's see if you answer that one.

Pia
[age 8]

Dear God,
My mom and my father are divorced. For 3 years.
Nobody's perfect. But why did you pick us? I wish
we were all with each other.
Maybe you could have them get along on
weekends.

> Please,
> Stephen
> [age 11]

Dear God,
I learned in school that you can make butter flies
out of caterpilars. I think that's cool. What can you
do for my sister? She's ugly.
Please don't tell my parents I wrote you.

> Your buddy,
> Greg
> [age 11]

"Do You Spend Your Spear Time with the Israelites, God?"

Holy God,

When someone you know does not have enough money $$$, should you ask him if he needs help? I could not find this in the parables.

Oh it is for pineapple bubble gum.

Love,
Your pal al
[age 9]

God,

I know a kid at school. His name is Tom Chen. He is Chinese. Most of us are not. Boy you like to have variety.

Love,
Andy
[age 10]

Dear God,

Be my friend? It won't cost you nothing and you don't even have to perform too many miracles.

William
[age 8]

Dear God,

I think that you are swell. My priest said that we are wrong if we think that you are only in the clouds. He says you are here on earth too.

If it is okay with my mother, would you like to come over to dinner on Tuesday night?

We are having lasanye!

> Hope you can make it,
> Madelyn
> [age 9]

Dear God,

I feel that Jesus is a friend of mine. Since he's your friend too, that makes us friends. Right or not? Let's get together to play sometime. You can bring all the toys you have and I'll bring mine. We'll see who has more.

> Love,
> Lori
> [age 7]

Dear God,

On earth as it is in heaven. You and my friend Cindy are the best.

Love,
Carol
[age 10]

Dear God. God of Justice.

I hate to bother you but there's this kid. His name is Billy Forte. He's always bothering me and being mean. He tried to steal my glove. Can you rub him out!!!

Sorry to bug you,
John
[age 8]

Dear God,
My girlfriends and I started the God Fan Club. Would you like to buy a button? We're going to make them ourselves.
Just so you know, here are the members so far.
Tracy, Mary, Me, Lynn, Paula, and You
Love, Sue
[age 8]

Dear God,
I live in Maine. I have a lot of friends here. People here are great.
Some people say we talk funny. That makes me mad. They should talk. They are from Boston.
Love,
Amanda
[age 8]
My mother's friends live in Boston.

Long Distance to GOD:
I hope that you are well . . .
And taking care of the world. Please make us
friendly with all the Arabs, with the eastern peoples
and with the Africaners.
And please, this is important. Make me friends
with Johnny Martins. We do not get along.

Alphonse
[age 10]

Dear God,
O hello God. I love music and so do my friends.
We sing in the church choir together. Please make
sure we always stay friends. Help us to sing better.

Judith
[age 11]

Dear God,

Why couldn't anyone in Israel get along in the Bible? There was always stone throwing and fighting. Jake, Joseph, Abe, Moses—you name them. No person was the friend of another. That's no good.

Roy
[age 10]

Dear God,

My baseball team went 5 and 15 last year. That means we lost 15 times. I hurt a lot about this. Please say a prayer for us.

Thanks,
Kevin
[age 9]

My friend Sam is on the team too. He's nice but he strikes out a lot.

Dear God old pal,

How's it going man? Can you fix it so my friends and me can stay out later in the summer.

We are cool.

Mark
[age 11]

Dear God,

Who was Mohammed? Was he a friend of yours like Jesus?

Also, were Moses and Joshua friends or just business partners?

I'm taking a class on
religions,
Fanny
[age 12]

Dear Gods,
All the kids on my block have 3 Speeds. You wouldn't want me to be left out . . . So
Merry Christmas ahead of
time,
Bob
[age 9]

Dear God,
Did you ever play 4 Squares with the other gods in heaven. We play it here on my block.
Maybe you play 4 Halos or something.
Love and kisses,
Dana
[age 8]

Dear God,

I am having fun and making friends. Dave is talking to me about things you do and say. But I told him. How should I know? Ask my friend George. He gets A's in school and I get C's!

Sorry,
Joe
[age 9]

Dear God,

You are a good friend to me when I am in need. Like maybe now. I am broke.

Your buddy,
Howard
[age 12]

Dear God,

Best regards. I am going to go play with my girl-friends after this. I am going to tell them about the stuff I just talked about and about the banner and pencils that the man gave me.

If you told him what to buy for the kids, thank you. You have good taste.

Heather
[age 9]

Dear God,

I found out that I have to get glasses. I am worried about what my friends will say. They may tease me and say 4 eyes. Please make sure they do not.

I am not vain or anything.

Carmen
[age 9]

Dear friendly God,
I think you are like a regular person.
I do not believe those people who say you are dead or far away.
You probabaly live on the next street.

> Marcy,
> [age 8]

Dear God,
I just made a new friend today.
His name is Dave Heller. He is white and I am black but that is fine.
We both love basketball.

> Love,
> Bill the thrill
> [age 9]

Jesus,
You and me is tight.

> I luv you,
> Richard
> [age 6]

To God,
   Who do you spend your spear time with?
   The Israelites?

                   Ken
                   [age 12]

"Do You Watch All of Us People on a Big TV Screen?"

Dear GOD,

I think there is much too many things about money these days. Especially on television.

You should take some money away from people so it would not be such a big deal.

Don't tell them
who gave you the idea,
Susie
[age 7]

Dear God,

Do you watch television?

Or do you just see Earth on a big screen?

Do you have a channel for Forest Hills in New York? That is where I live.

Let me know when you
will be watching so that I
can dress up,
Sybil
[age 11]

Dear God,

Channel 4 has a nice peacock on its ads. I bet you watch them. Peacocks are in the bible, my minister says.

Take it slow,
Dennis
[age 9]

Dear God,

Do your kids watch cartoons on Saturdays? Or are they helping you get ready for church on Sunday?

Your friend,
Ted
[age 7]

Dear God,

What's your best sport? Mine is basketball. I like the Pistons. I guess you don't, since they don't win much. Do you get ESPN?

Tim
[age 11]

Hey, God,

Do you know how in commercials they say they are going to take a break to bring us a word from the sponsor?

Well you should do that with people in their homes because you are everybody's sponsor. That would be neat. That way you could communicate with the people.

Stay Cool,
Riley
[age 12]

Dear God,

My mom always says that my brother and me would like to stay up so late that we may as well stay up for Sermonette.

She says it is a religious show. Are you the host? Are you like David Letterman?

What time are you on,
Risa
[age 8]

Dear God,

What is your top magazine if you read them? I think they are all sleazy, besides Seventeen. Maybe you like Time. My dad reads that and, beside, you created time so they got the idea from you.

Love,
Louise
[age 11]

Dear God,

Is Krypton a real place? Maybe it is just a place in Hollywood.

Frank
[age 9]

Dear God,

What do you think about all those movies about you around Easter time? I think they're kind of corny, myself.

Your buddy,
Charles
[age 9]

Dear God,

Can't you do something about all the bad news on TV? I always change the chanell.

Cindy
[age 7]

Dear God,

"Highway to Heaven" is my favorite show. Do you help write it?

Love,
Alice
[age 9]

Dear God.

I wonder if you could help me out. My mom and dad said I can't watch TV for a week. So I guess I'm going to miss all those religious shows, unless you do something. How about putting in a good word for me?

Love,
Matt
[age 7]

Dear God,

I think the "Today" show is corny. I watch it sometimes before I catch the bus to school.

You should do the "Tomorrow" show. It would be good because you know the future. All the people would watch. I bet your ratings would be out of this world.

Best wishes,
Roger
[age 11]

Dear God,

They could have more bible stories on TV. I recommend the King Solomon story, Moses, Jesus, and the lady who turned into salt.

The Flood might make it difficult. It would be hard to show and the kids might not watch. Plus there would not be enough parts for people. Just animals.

With love,
Roberto
[age 9]

Dear God,

What do you get paid? My dad says the guy who reads the news on Channel 2 (CBS) gets paid more than you.

Why don't they give you a big raise?

I care,
Jamie
[age 11]

Dear God,

Do you and Mr. Rogers talk to each other. He is very wise.

Love,
Anthony
[age 6]

Dear God,
   A lot of folks say there is too much rough stuff on TV and too much killing too.
   I say there is too much rough and tough stuff and killing in the Bible.

                    Make my day,
                    Derek
                    [age 11]

"There Isn't Any School in Heaven, Is There?"

Dear Jesus,

How did you learn all that stuff in the Book by Luke without going to school much?

Sharon
[age 7]

Dear God,

I read about Abraham in school. Why did you give him such a hard time before you let him become a teacher?

The teachers here got it easy.

Barry
[age 9]

Dear God,

You don't have to spell real good to get into heaven, do you?

My teacher told us that when we meet St. Peter we have to spell a word like exaggerate. If you get it right, you go to heaven. If you're wrong, you go down stairs.

I don't mean the principils office.

Sincerely,
Dom
[age 10]

Dear God,

I am a Christian Scientist person. In school I am in the third grade. We learn about many religions but not ours. Are you prejudiced or something?

I want to know,
Alicia
[age 9]

Dear New Testament God,

Since you like to write so much, maybe you could write my current events term paper for me. It could be about anything—even you!

I am desparate,
Raymond
[age 12]

Dear God,

Did you invent math to count the animals on Noah's ark? Do we still need it?

Jeanne
[age 11]

Dear God,

Help. I have a favor to ask you. Mr. Arene teaches us. He is pretty strictly mean. I think he does not go to church either.

I wonder if you could send Jesus or an angel down to talk with him. Maybe I could invite Jesus in for my history project. That way Mr. Arene won't expect anything.

End of letter,
Orson
[age 12]

Dear God,

My people believe in Islam. Most of the other people at school do not. I live in Masachusetts.

Can you put more Islamic people in schools and houses in Masachusetts.

Thank you.
Ahmed
[age 12]

Dear God,
Hi from School. No message.
Love,
Carla
[age 6]

Dear God,
My mom says that I can only stay out after school till it gets dark.
My question is: Can you make the sun stand still?
I figured if you did it once you could probaly do it again.
Freddie
[age 11]

Dear God,
Did Matthew and John have to go to college?
Back here in grade 4,
Art
[age 10]

Dear God,

I love school and I try my best all the time. I also say my prayers every night.

I hope this counts when it's my turn to be judged.

A good Christian,
Gloria
[age 11]

God and who all is listening.

MAKE SCHOOL ONLY AN HOUR A DAY!

A good student
[age 7]

Dear God,

Did you make pencils and pens just like you made men and girls.

I think pencils and pens go together better.

Your friend,
Charles
[age 12]

Dear heavenly father, (God)

I pray to you each and every night. Sometimes I pray to you during Science—this is not good for my grades.

Davida
[age 11]

Dear God,

Are Hebrew schools better than regular schools? I know that you must be Jewish, but try to be honest.

Hello,
Linda
[age 8]

Dear God,

I hate gym. I bet Sarah and Rachel and Becky did not have to do gym stuff in the Bible.

Boy those were the days.

Love and prayers,
Naomi
[age 10]

Dear God,

When you threw Adam and Eve and all the others out of the garden, that must be when you started to have schools. You must have been plenty mad.

Hope this gives you a laugh,
David
[age 9]

Dear God,

My dad is a professor in college. They have all the knowledge in the world there.

If you are in Michigan, its ok if you use the library.

Working hard,
Sally
[age 8]

Dear sweet and friend God,

I am being very good. I am good to my mom, my dad, my brother Bill, and my sister Elizabeth. I am nice to my friends like you. I am nice to my grandma and grandpa too.

I am *even* nice to my teachers. I try to forgiving them for being so boring.

Love,
Kristen
[age 8]

Dear God,

I am going to begin junior high next year. You helped me make it so far. Do not leave me now!

Please,
Les
[age 12]

Dear God,

I would like to know if you are like the principle of a school and all the presidents and kings are like teachers.

Andrea
[age 7]

Dear God,

I am doing police for you.

My english teacher, Mrs. Clayburn, has pointed ears.

I think she is Satin.

Keep me covered,
George
[age 8]

Dear God,

We read that you made a bush burn to the ground and you did not use matches. Wow. I would like to see this done to my school.

Yea,
Timmy
[age 10]

GOD
1 NORTH POLE
EARTH 7777

How is it up there where you are?

I learned about you in geography. Say hi to Santa Claus.

Bea
[age 9]

Dear God,

We learn about you a lot in Sunday school. We heard that you don't like temples with money in it and that you don't like Romans much either.

Who do you like?

Signed Bill,
I am easy to like
[age 10]

Dear God,

How far did you get in school?

I stayed back last year and I am worried.

Tyler
[age 10]

Dear God,

Thank you for helping the poor people all around the world and for helping to educate them too.

That must be hard work. Do your kids help or are they too busy doing they're homework?

Love,
Cherie

Dear God,

Do you have schools in heaven or are the angels and servants born smart?

Doris
[age 11]

"Is There a Special Place in Heaven for Cabbage Patch Kids?"

Dear God,

Hockey is pretty tough but I love it.

I always say a prayer for all the players' injuries after the games.

Kevin
[age 12]

Jesus,

I feel very near to you.

I feel like you are beside me all the time.

Please be with me on Thursday. I am running in a 3 mile race then. I will need all the speed in the world. If are not busy with other things, maybe you could be at the starting line, the finish line, and everywhere in between.

Frankie
[age 11]

Dear God,

Were you a BOY Scout? I am.

Did you ever camp out in the desert and play jokes on people in the Bible? I bet you did.

We do all the time and have a blast.

Nat the rat
[age 10]

Dear God,

I am fond of you. No question about it.

I love to cook. Today, I would like to make something for You. How about an omelette with bread and butter. I'll put lots of cheese in it.

Do you eat bacon? I don't know since I am a Christian. You might be kosher or something.

Love,
Melissa Sue
[age 11]

Dear Dear Dear God,
I see you in my dreams all the time.
I know it is you because you have a crown on and you are always fishing.
Say hello next time.
Love,
Craig
[age 9]

Dear God,
If you think it was cool the way Jesus walked on the water, you should watch me water ski!
Steve
[age 12]

Dear Jesus,
Since you retired two thousands years ago what kinds of things do you do?
Maybe you should try bowling or you could sing in a church group like my grandmother does.
Your friend,
Pam
[age 9]

Dear God,

My mom tells me a story about you every night. Last night she told me about how you always remember your mother on her birthday. And you give her divine gifts.

I think she was kidding me and herself.

Love,
Holden
[age 7]

Dear God,

Do you have toy spaceships and things like that? That must be fun, but hard to keep track of.

You should always put your toys away when you are done.

Randy
[age 8]

Dear God, of Bible fame,

Do you know me? I carry an American Express card. Just kidding. Guess what. I'm going on a trip to California next month.

I guess you know that already.

> Hope your miracles are
> good ones,
> Ernie
> [age 11]

Dear God,

Was building car models big when you were a kid? Or whatever they called you.

> Warren
> [age 7]

Dear God,

Do you have a special place for Cabbage Patch kids in heaven? Are they closer to you because they come from nature?

> Love,
> Angela
> [age 8]

Dear God,

I like to read a lot. We read *The Great Gatsby* in school. Do you have time to read? I bet you like religious books and biographers.

Please write me back,
Terry
[age 12]

Dear God,

I have a big collection of dolls. Sometimes I play Bible with them. I have them act your stories. Once I had them do the ten plagues. Then I had them go in the desert. I was not too rough on them.

Hi,
Charlotte
[age 9]

Dear God,

Do you ever get bored? I do. Do you get into trouble then? Is that why you started thunder and rain?

Let me know,
Paula
[age 11]

Dear God,

Thanks for the Air Jordans for Christmas. You must be a basketball fan like me. What do you wear, Air Moses? We have a Moses here too, but he's big and he plays for the NBA!

Your humble star,
Ron
[age 12]

Dear God,

Want to hear a joke? What is red, very long, and you hear it right before you go to sleep? Give up? Answer is a *sermon*.

Your friend,
Frank
[age 11]

Dear God,

I just learned how to play chess. Does the earth look like a chessboard to you?

Libby
[age 11]

God,

I need to confess. I am sorry but I looked at my older brother Eddie's *Playboy* magazine. I didn't really like it though.

> Sorry,
> George
> [age 10]

God, when do you think it would be okay to start going out with girls?

Dear God,

What do you think of Hulk Hogan? Wrestling is fake. Isn't it?

> Thanks for the inside
> story,
> Carol
> [age 8]

Dear God,

I just want to say hi! And thanks for all the people you are helping who are starving.

I'm okay here. But there is one thing. I love tennis very much and it is hard to get a court around here. Can you build some more in my neighborhood?

Thank you,
Erica
[age 8]

Dear God,

When I get to high school I want to be captain of the cheerleaders. Please help me make the team.

You would like the school. It's Catholic.

Mary Ellen,
[age 12]

Dear God,

I wonder if we have a lot in common. Do you like the Beach Boys? I do. I live near the Pacific Ocean.

From the west coast,
Amanda
[age 10]

Dear God,

Art is my favorite subject. I want to draw you a picture of you. Here goes.

I need to work on details. It would help if you could come down so that I could get a look at you.

Michael
[age 7]

Dear God,

I love to eat. Thanks for all the food. Pizza was the best idea you had.

Ralph
[age 7]

"What Did Adam and Eve Do for Fun?"

Dear God,

What is the rest of the story about when you made boys and girls? There must be a reason why you made two different brands of people.

Hank
[age 6]

Dear God,

When do you think it's okay to start dating? How old were you when you went out with Mrs. God? Did you kiss her on the first date?

Your friend,
Cheryl
[age 10]

Dear God,

Do you think there's enough love these days? I feel there's a shortage.

Love,
Ken
[age 9]

Dear God,

I have a crush on a boy in my class (third grade). His name is Ralph. Do you know him? I'm a little scared. So I wonder if you could do a check on him.

Best regards,
Ellen
[age 9]

Dear God,

I go to a Catholic school. The priests there are very nice. But did you ever think of giving these men different clothes. I think the nuns can stay the same.

Curious,
Mary Jo
[age 10]

Dear God,

How involved do you get in marriages? Do you give the couples any time alone?

Just asking,
Wayne
[age 12]

Dear God,
   I went to my cousin's wedding last week. I heard that you were there. I must have missed you. Do you get to all the weddings or do you just pick some? You must eat a lot of cake.
                              Love,
                              Alexandria
                              [age 10]

God,
   I am a nice girl. I am glad I am not a boy. They are ugly. Only Jesus was nice.
                              Love,
                              Andrea
                              [age 6]

Dear God,

What do you think of people who act sexy? I think they are kidding themselves. It is better to act like you really are.

I try to act religious. I do my best.

Trying hard,
Brandon
[age 9]

Dear God,

When you made love was it hard to plan?

Is that why girls and guys act so goofy when they go out?

With many times love,
Brett
[age 9]

Dear God,

I read about Miriam and Moses. Boy she was a good sister to him.

I hope that he appreciated her. Some men don't.

Amy
[age 10]

Dear God,

I'm writing to complain about how men get the biggest say in everything. I want this to stop. Now.

I want to be President some day and things are going to change. We're going to need a tornado or a hurricane or something.

I will let you know,
Linda
[age 11]

Dear God,

Why do boys like dirt so much? I think it might have been better if you got the people out of the desert sooner.

Candy
[age 8]

Dear God,

Do women in heaven dress up and wear makeup or are they just down to earth people?

I'd like to know,
Wendy
[age 10]

Dear God,

Why do men and girls always fight? Did you believe that the earth would be more interesting that way?

John
[age 8]

Dear God,

When Jonah was in the whale was it a he whale or a she whale. I think girls are probably fatter.

Mike
[age 7]

Dear God,

I'm glad that you are a man. If you were not, you might not have made boys.

I am a boy,
Darren
[age 10]

Dear God,

I think if you were a woman you would be more involved with domestic things like cooking and cleaning. And sewing.

Karen Ann
[age 9]

Dear God,

I read about how Delilah cut Samson's hair. Is that why there are so many female hairdressers?

Warren
[age 10]

God,

What did Adam and Eve do for fun? My mom said they played with toys and ate but I know better.

Chris
[age 9]

Dear God,
   Girls are weird. Except for my mom.
                    Love you,
                    Timmy
                    [age 7]

Dear God,
   Why do we always have to let the girls go first? I
bet they did not want to go first when the Christians
were killed in the stadiums.
                    Carl
                    [age 10]

Dear God,
   When you were small, did you always listen to
your mom? Women think they know everything but
they do not.
   I bet if you listened you would not be so big and
powerful today. That is a fact.
                    Hello God,
                    Bryn
                    [age 9]

Dear Ms. God:

I believe that you are a woman. In fact I am sure for sure. I think that is why the rivers and sky and birds are so beautiful.

If by some flook you are a boy please do not take it out on me. Boys should not hit girls.

Trisha
[age 11]

"Volcanoes Are Cool, But You Should Watch Your Temper, God!"

Dear God,

Do angels do carpentry and plumbing in the sky? If you don't have to be too handy, I would like to apply.

Yours,
Carmen
[age 8]

To the Lord,

I don't buy that evolution stuff.
I think that you did the whole thing by yourself.

Scott
[age 9]

Dear God,

I used to want to be an astronaut. But I'm not sure it's safe anymore. What's the weather report?

Kevin
[age 12]

Dear God,

I think that you are wonderful. When you invented snow, did you know that people would use it for skiing?

Love,
Amy
[age 10]

Dear God,

Next time you send a flood, could you please send me a telegram beforehand? Mostly, I've been good.

Waiting to hear,
Ted
[age 12]

Dear God,

Do you have a giant computer or do you count all the people of the world on your fingers?

Love,
William
[age 6]

Dear God,
   I am a big fan of yours and Einstein's, God.
I think that you are both very smart.
But he made bombs and you try to stop them.
That is better.

Jan
[age 10]

Dear God,
   Why didn't you make cars earlier, God? That way the Jews could have good speed and gotten away from the Egyptians' land faster and David could have made a clean get away from Goliath.

Your friend,
Theresa
[age 9]

Dear God,

When you had birds fly south for winter did you think people would too?

We are going to Florida for February vacation!

Love,
Patricia
[age 10]

Dear God,

Do you feel that the scientists and the presidents are to blame for nuclear weapons or are you willing to take on the responsability your self?

Jerome
[age 12]

Mr. God,

I think it is amazing the way everything fits together in the world. Look at heat in our houses, the moon, the sun and rain so farmers' plants will grow.

How do you do it? Mirrors?

Judy,
[age 11]

Dear God,

Volcanoes are cool. But you should learn to control your temper (that is what my mother always says to me).

Love,
Victor
[age 11]

Dear God,

I learned that when it is 1 o'clock here it is a different time in China. Why? Did you want to keep us guessing?

Sincerely,
Ellen
[age 9]

God,

Is a hail storm a big God sneeze? Bless you.

Terrence
[age 8]

Dear God,

Thank you for all the great food that we can grow.
My two favorite foods are watermelon and ice
cream (rocky road).

It would be great if by 2000, we could grow ice
cream (at least vanilla, chocolate, and rocky road).

If you are planning on making some changes that
would be a good one.

Love,
Mel
[age 10]

Dear God in the heavens,

I am flying to New Orleans next week with my
family. We are going to something called Marti
Gras.

I will look for you on the way.

Love always,
Sharona
[age 9]

Dear God,
Did you make it so cold in Michigan because you thought we could take it? Or was it a practical joke of yours?

I ain't laughin,
Eric!
[age 11]

GOD
God's Lab
Earth to God. Earth to God. Come in God.
POW. POW.
Hey God. Let's play making things. Let's make a radar station. Then let's make a new kind of plane. It will have supersonic hearing. That way it can catch hijackers. They will have to report to the devil then.

Tim
[age 10]

Dear God,

I live in Michigan. I heard a song that says it don't rain in a place called Indianapolis. I heard that it isn't far away. Why don't you let it rain there?

Tim
[age 7]

Dear God,

What I want to know is—where do people go when they die? My dad says you go to Russia if you're not good. I don't think so because it's too cold there.

Yours truly,
Andrew
[age 9]

Dear God,

I think it's unbelievable the way you made thunder and lightning bolts. We like the way you make lightning bolts so much, we put them on our football uniforms! I play for the Chargers.

Dan
[age 11]

Dear God,
I'm in the fifth grade and we have to do a science fair project. We can get help from a grownup (honest). I think maybe you would be ok. Can you help me out?

Help,
Diane
[age 11]

Dear God,
I heard that you can predict the future. Are you better than a horoscope? What do you think I'm going to ask for next Christmas?

Best wishes,
Susan
[age 11]

Dear God,

I love you. I love the way you made the sky and the sun.

One thing I wondered though. Doesn't it get kind of hot up there near the sun?

We are air conditioned so we are O K.

Love,
Deirdre
[age 8]

To God,

My question is this one. Did you create all the oceans at once or add when you needed it?

Was the Pacific hard to do?

Ronny
[age 8]

Dear God,
    Have you ever wondered if you made a mistake?
    Do you think may be it would have been better to do babies different?
    I mean look at all the trouble it has made.

Let me Know,
Leon
[age 12]

"Is That Khadafy Guy Like Pharoah in the Bible?"

Dear Mr. God,

Why don't you have girls fight in wars? Even in the Bible they didn't. You'd think that because they are hard to get along with, they would be good at fighting!

Just an idea,
Marty
[age 10]

Dear God,

I want to suggest a thing.

More Peace!

While I have your atention, I would also like to ask for a pair of Reebok sneakers for Christmas.

Thank you, I love you,
Caroline
[age 11]

Dear GOD,

Please help the Democats and the Republicans to get along. That way we could get along with other places too. Like Russia and the Arabs and the Vietnams.

Thanks,
Clark
[age 10]

Dear God,

Please make all the people on the earth better to each other. That means no more terrorism and violence like on tv.

I want to say thanks for that you are trying to do.

Best wishes,
Anita
[age 11]

Dear God,

Why did you make it so there is always to sides to things, good guys and bad guys, east and west? We are all the same. Aren't we?

Truly,
Ken
[age 12]

Dear God,

I read in the paper about the summit with the Russians.

Is that anything like the summit in Houston?

Bill
[age 9]

Dear God,

When I grow up will I have to fight in the army? Will there be a war?

I'm not chicken or anything. I just want to know in advance.

Terry
[age 10]

Dear God,

If Jesus was alive today what country would you send him to? I recommend the US of A. We really need him.

Love,
Edward, Jr.
[age 11]

Dear God,

Was there a China in your day? Did you know Marcus Polo?

Ted
[age 8]

Dear God,

Do you try to avoid Russia when you travel?

Love,
Sharon
[age 7]

Dear God,
Is that Khadafy guy like Pharoah in the Bible or is he worst?

Your fan,
Alex
[age 8]

Dear God,
My family and me went to Germany last summer. We stopped at those camp places were a lot of people died.
My question is—did you know about this? Were you away then?

Please answer when you can,
Cindy Ellen
[age 11]

Dear God,

The bomb is not such a hot invention. Maybe you should recall it.

Love,
Margaret
[age 12]

Dear God,

My family and I are practicing Catholics. The stuff in North Ireland bothers us a lot. I don't know if your Irish or not. Maybe you could help though.

Sincerely,
Kathleen
[age 10]

Dear General God,

Boy, you sure do have a lot of wars here. We learned in history about World Wars I and II. Then there was the korean war. I don't know much about that. Then there was Vietnam. Now there always seem to be some fighting going on.

I figure we must be sergeants to you. You must want things this way. Otherwise it would not have been like that in the Bible too. And there was plenty of WAR there too.

Andy
[age 10]

Dear God,

That was a cool trick with the slingshot.

Dave
[age 10]

Dear God,

Could you talk to the Sihks and Hindus. I am Hindu but I live in America. I have family far away. I don't want to see them harmed.

In case you don't know, America is not too far from Canada.

> With love and
> kindness,
> Mahua
> [age 9]

Dear God,

I saw a poster in a store that went like this:

WAR IS BAD FOR KIDS AND OTHER LIVING THINGS LIKE THAT

As a kid i feel it is my duty to tell you about this. If you have not seen it you should. You can get it at Woolworth's.

> One of the kids,
> Sandy
> [age 10]

Dear Jesus,
Are we related?
My two uncles have beards. Maybe we are. (They are in the army though.)
Love,
Francine
[age 7]

Dear God,
At church my minister talks a lot about throwing stones and sins. Any idea what he means?
I think you must know. I don't get the hang of this stuff.
A regular church-goer,
Artie
[age 11]

"Is There a Christmas in Russia, God?"

Dear God, Jesus, Mary, or who ever is there,

I have always wondered. Do people in far off places like Syria and Arabia have Christmas?

If they do not what do they think they are doing when they eat turkey and stuffing and sing carols.

Happy New Years,
Troy
[age 7]

Dear God,

What do bunnies have to do with Easter?
Why don't you have camels instead?

I will let you know if I
think of anything else to
do.
Brian
[age 10]

Dear Santa,

I was going to write God but I heard that you were in charge of toys.

Love ♡ ♡ ♡
Brooke
[age 6]

Dear God,

We learned in school about a book called the koran. Do they do that one at Easter Vigil or something?

I am curious,
Charlotte
[age 12]

Dear God,

Do you have a Christmas tree or a whole (maybe holy) forest? It must be hard to light it all up.

Danny
[age 9]

Dear Jesus,

I want to thank you for going up there on the Cross for us every Good Fridays.

You must be real happy when the weekend is over.

Thanks,
Anita
[age 11]

Dear God,
   Easter is eggsactly what I would have created.
                    Loren
                    [age 11]

Dear God,
   My favorite Christmas song is Rudolf.
   What's yours?
   I bet you like jingle bells. That one is a lot older.
                    Jordan
                    [age 6]

Dear God,

I like your signs.
                    Love,
                    Maria
                    [age 5]

Dear God,

Here is five things I would like to see changed.
Number 1—Mass
Number 2—Bad nuns
Number 3—War
Number 4—Television
Number 5—Make Christmas every week.

I could be your agent,
Donny
[age 12]

Dear God,

Did the Jews start Chanukah to go along with Christmas or did something really happen back there in the ancient days?

My friend told me about that lamp story. That was pretty good.

Best wishes,
Steve
[age 12]

Dear God,
Was Jesus born in a manger because there was no
Holiday Inns in those years?

Only kidding,
Your pal Ricky
[age 10]

Dear God,
My bat mitzvah is only nine months away. Please
think about me.
I hope we can meet. I'll be the red-haired girl who
looks scared.

Shana
[age 12]

Dear Special Person,

Thank you for Christmas, Easter, and for summer. Also thanks for being with me.

My next birthday is July 16. Mark it down.

> You are neat,
> Ryan
> [age 7]

DEAR God,

Did you put All Saints Day near Holloween to give all the sides an equal chance? Hah hah.

> I am going to be a monk
> on Holloween. Fooled
> you.
> Fitz
> [age 11]

Dear Hashem,

As you probably know I am Jewish.

I am small for my age. I way only 76 pounds.

Is it okay if I don't fast all the way on Yom Kippur?

> This would help,
> Jay
> [age 10]

I would like to have only soda and potato chips for energy, maybe?

Dear God,

What is franks and cents? Was it an old kind of money?

> Maybe it was food?
> Todd
> [age 7]

Dear God,

In the Holy Land, what do you do about snow for Christmas? That must be different and kind of weird.

Love ya God,
Bobby
[age 9]

Dear God,

Is there a Christmas in Russia?
They got nerve. They must have stole it from us.

Mad, real mad
Jimmy K.
[age 11]

Dear Sky God,

Do you have holidays on the moon?
I bet you eat lots of cheese there with dinner.

Captain Kirk
[age 12]

Santa Claus, the reindeer, and God,

I am going to catch you. I am going to make you stay for cereal and milk.

I like Lucky Charms. You can have Cherios. Rudolph can have red cereal.

See you,
Alex
[age 5]

My mom helped me spell this.

Dear God—Who I believe In.

Do you celebrate July 4 or do you just go wild on religion holidays?

If you do not you should.

We have a picnic here.

Carey
[age 10]

Dear God,

For Thanksgiving do you have a big deal in heaven? Or something else. Or do you just visit somebody's family in New England?

> You can come here,
> Elizabeth
> [age 9]

Dear God,

I know my mother and father give the things on Xmas, but I still think you must be the inspiration. Thanks. Keep giving them ideas.

> Yours truly, at Xmas and
> always,
> Danielle
> [age 12]

Dear God,

Why don't you put Columbus in the Bible? (We get it off from school?)

Was it because he traveled a lot and this made it hard to get the story write?

Samantha
[age 9]

Dear God,

What is a Greek Orthodox?

I hear they have a different year than we have. How can that be?

Do you cover them too?

Felicia
[age 10]

Dear God,

Is it a big letdown for you after Christmas? What about Santa?

What do you do on new years eve and the day too? Or is that old hats to you buy now after a million years?

Carlton
[age 10]

Dear God,

I think it is really cool the way you made such a big day for your son and had the whole world give gifts and all. But I think you should be fair and have days for the apostels too.

Petermas   Paulmas   Andymas

Even Judasmas would be good. Everyone should get a *2ND* chance.

Merry Christmas,
Andy
[age 11]

Dear God,

SHALOM. Last Passover we ate Matzoh on everything. I mean Everything.

Couldn't we just eat toast? SHALOM.

Your good girl,
Sari
[age 9]

Dear God,

You are the best.

Easter is the best holiday.

Jesus's resurrection is the best story. I saw it in a movie once. It was the best vampire movie I ever saw.

Love,
Arn
[age 7]

Dear God,

I am Lutheran and two of my best friends are Jewish. One other is different all together. He is from India.

I think that it is not right that you left them out of Christmas. Please put them back in. They are very kind to me.

—Love always—
Ann
[age 9]

"Could You Please Change the Taste of Asparagus, God?"

Dear God,

Do you have telephones in heaven? My number is 555-6392. What is yours? I get home from school about three-thirty everyday.

I'll talk to you,
Martha
[age 8]

Dear Creator,

I think the best thing you ever invented was cartoons. All the kids I know love 'em.

Hello from Detroit,
Dan
[age 7]

Dear God,

My dad drinks beer. It looks kind of gross. Did King Solomon drink beer?

Stanley,
[age 10]

Dear God,
    DON'T GIVE UP ON US AND WE WON'T
FORGET ABOUT YOU.
                        Anonymous,
                        [age 11]

Dear God, Mary, and Family,
    Merry Christmas to all of you and all your rela-
tives. That means Jesus and Peter too.
                        Love,
                        Cynthia Sykes
                        12 Treadmill Road
                        [age 7]

To God/Send it Federal Express
    Hope this gets to you by 1999. Otherwise I get my
stamp back. Guaranteed!
                        Your pen pal,
                        Dawn
                        [age 11]

Dear God,

I have doubts about you sometimes. Sometimes I really believe. Like when I was four and I hurt my arm and you healed it up fast. But my question is, if you could do this why don't you stop all the bad in the world? Like war. Like diseases. Like famine. Like drugs.

And there are problems in other people's neighborhoods too.

I'll try to believe more,
Ian
[age 10]

Dear God,

YOU ARE FANTASTIC!!!! Send me your autograph. Write it to

To my favorite person in America, who is the handsomest and smartest too, who all the girls want.

Over and out,
Bert
[age 9]

Sign it with a great big ⊂ and a lightning bolt. So all the kids will believe it's really you.

Dear God,

What do you think of kings and queens like Prince Charles and Queen Di?

I think they are snobs, if you ask me.

> No hard feelings,
> Ernie
> [age 11]

Dear God,

Can you get me into a soap opera?

> Love and kisses,
> Betty
> [age 8]

Dear God in heaven,

Thank you so much for helping my two years old brother stop peaing in his pants. My whole family is relieved!

> Thank you,
> Lorissa
> [age 6]

Dear "God,"

How did you get the name Earth? Ever think of changing it?

I'd like to see it called Tom's World.

Tom
[age 11]

Dear God,

Do you believe in spirits and ghosts? What about things in outer space? I don't but my friend Ed says their all around. I think Ed is weird.

Your friend too,
Robert
[age 11]

Dear God,

Could you change the taste of asparagus? Everything thing else is OK.

Love,
Fred
[age 9]

Dear God,
In the beginning of everything, you said let there be light. Right? How did this feel? I would like to know.

It must have been strange to have night all the time. Like in Alaska. But I guess you must have been used to it. What made you turn the switch?

I live in (Connecticut.) Please keep the light here.

Thank you,
Arlene
[age 8]

Dear Big God,
I think that you look like a big monster. But you do good things for people. Like feasts and famine.

You make me laugh,
Diane
[age 10]

Dear God,
My mother said we used to eat fish on Fridays.
Did you stop it because of the smell?

Very truly yours,
Christa
[age 11]

Dear God and Jesus,
I'm a big follower of you guys. I root for you both
all the time. Keep those miracles coming.

Your best friend,
Stephen
[age 8]

Dear God,

Hello.

I hate people who say too much.

Emily
[age 10]

To Whom It May Concern,

I want to believe in you real hard. But I don't know how. My mom does but my dad does not. How can I know for sure? Why don't you make things easier? It would be nice. Nothing special. You don't have to part the sea or nothing. Just something easy.

Like have me turn thirteen sooner.

Joan
[age 12]

Dear God,

I saw the Grand Canyon last summer. Nice piece of work.

Love,
Alan
[age 9]

Dear GOD,
   I think that you very kind and generous.
   Can you see if I can get a bigger allowance?
                              Mike
                              [age 11]

Dear God,
   I don't really believe in you but I'm supposed to
write a letter so here goes.
   Also I want to get in a book.
   If you are real why don't you prove it by appearing
to me?
   I'll be on Schoolhouse Road at 5 O'CLOCK to-
morrow.
   We'll see.
                              Laura
                              [age 9]

Dear Lord,
    You and I have something in common.
    We both have a lot of names.
    You have Lord
                God
                Jesus
                Father.
                            Signed,
                            Rodney William Peter
                            Johnson, Junior
                            [age 8]
Please look ━━━━━━▶ I also have a nickname. It
                            is Rodent.
                            What's yours?

Dear God,
    In school we read all there about Jesus being
born.
    One part I did not understand.
    What is a mackulet decepsion?
                            Love,
                            Phyllis
                            [age 10]

Dear Only God,
   You light up my life. So do mom and dad.

I hope you like this. I am not sure what it means.	Luv, Toni [age 7]

Dear God,
   Thank you for sending Doctor Heller to ask me questions about you. He is very nice and we are becoming friends now.
   But he looks too young to be a doctor. He looks more like an actor.
   Maybe he was in a Bible movie.

                    Love,
                    Connie
                    [age 10]

Dear God,

I read that home is where God (that's you) is.

What does that mean, I wonder?

Does it mean if I am at religious school I am not away from home?

Do I have to be in our living room to be with you?

Are you everywhere?

I am not sure. I just know that you are in my heart.

From home,
David
[age 12]

Dear God,

Did you know that our money says on it
IN YOU WE TRUST?

You must be rich.

Take it easy,
Your friend Jimmy
[age 9]

ABOUT THE AUTHOR

David Heller, Ph.D., is the author of fifteen books, including the bestselling gift books *Love Is Like a Crayon Because It Comes in All Colors* and *My Mother Is the Best Gift I Ever Got.* Additional books include: *Talking to Your Child About God, The Best Christmas Presents Are Wrapped in Heaven* and *Just Build the Ark and the Animals Will Come: Children on Bible Stories.*

Dr. Heller graduated *summa cum laude* from Harvard University and received his doctorate from the University of Michigan. His work has been featured on *20/20* and in *People, Cosmopolitan, Good Housekeeping, Catholic Digest, Woman's Day, Redbook, New Woman* and many other periodicals. His books have been translated into ten different languages.

He lives in Boston with his wife, Elizabeth.